PP

Something Like A Sonata

A Poet's Journal

Something Like A Sonata

A Poet's Journal

ALYSSA EVE

January 2016

It's Not Complicated

Sunday, January 3, 2016

This love I say
it's alive,
it's alive.

They say a great one
will keep you
wondering,
should you sail
or set it free
to get released
into the sea?

But we're alive,
we're alive
to live for today.

So when the past
comes to cage you in
keep an eye open
for a place
to descend
into the wild
where you belong.

Into the wild
where you belong
to live for today,

because you're alive
you survived
yesterday.

Political Affairs
Tuesday, January 19, 2016

So many decide to steep in war.

The personal type,
where the chemical ego
takes over the subject of self
and control's given to the loud charismatic.

It seems as if no matter how much time passes,
we find something to
take pride in fighting over,

and our priorities get so skewed,
we take precedence
in attacking each other's character
over settling our differences.

Yes, No, Maybe, I Don't Know
Thursday, January 21, 2016

At times life's a stranger,

at times

it's a mocking cover of our creation.

We live our lives in a photograph
where it seems a simple snap
will travel us around the world

and everyone wants to get famous
for who they've become
but everyone's so starved for attention.

At times, we become a stranger to ourselves.
We used to snap ourselves into a dusty box on the shelf,
become a distant memory,
then carry on into our futures.

It seems as if we're memorializing our lives
in stone as we go
and living in a state of nostalgia mourning.

Will we move on?
Have we lost ourselves?
Where's the line on the page?
Where's the space for us to be ourselves, to be free?
Where's the empty page to get filled with individuality?

It's as if we're victims of ourselves
and the pressure to post everything
for the world to see.

What happened to privacy?

We have the entire world at our fingertips
and rather than taking caution like we should,
we invite it into our homes
to destroy each bit of our well-being.

The price we pay for adoration
can be the cost of our self-esteem.

We Can't Change The World

Tuesday, January 26, 2016

The world's a circus,
or so it has become,
and we're either performers on a stage,
or watchers in the crowd
who stand in awe and disbelief.

Where contortionists not only twist their bodies,
but twist the truth.

Where acrobats go to great heights,
risk their lives and fall for you.

Where lion tamers make them jump
through flaming hoops,
then get stupid enough
to put their head in the lion's mouth.

The difference between the world and the circus,
a crowd large enough
has the power to stop the circus.

February 2016

What I Wish I Would've Said
Thursday, February 18, 2016

I don't know the secrets you hide today
and I hope, despite how hard today may become,
you're blessed with the courage
to break through this day
and the strength to live on until tomorrow.

A deep breath will do you good in your quiet times,
so take one, take two, take as many as you need.

Remember to slow down and enjoy
the little bit of life you have left in you.

When life caves in around you,
close your eyes and pray to God it's not the end.

Then when everything fails, fight for the life you've earned,
because you belong here,
and we need you here.

Sweet Dreams, Or Not. . .

Monday, February 22, 2016

I focus on my work tonight
with the worries of the clock
dancing in the back of my mind.

After each hour goes by,
the sun comes up,
and panic sets in
like my first attack happened yesterday.

So I put up blinds to block out the sun
behind my open eyes, with the fear of losing sleep,
if I can't see it,
it's not there,
right?

Why take a pill to end the anxiousness,
when delving deep into this task
would do the same?

I have days when I wish
I could function like everyone does,
and I have days when I do.

It's the persistent thought
which doesn't let my mind rest.

The thought which decides to come up with new ideas
as I start to doze off,
and robs me of any rest I should have had.

The eyes, wide open,
the entire night wasted
laying awake in a dark room
having conversations
with myself in my mind about
everything, nothing, and anything.

At times, I wish my mind
would slow down,
shut up,
and let me sleep.

Cut It Down
Friday, February 26, 2016

What
do you need to bury
in order to move on?

Half of you planted here,
while the other half
rooted itself deep in the past
in a dark place where you're unable
to see the faces
of those who care for you.

They don't care about your past
or cater to the guilt you have.

People worth calling friends
can be family
when the rest of the world
seems fed up with you;

when the last face you want to see
looks like your own,
look to their's for comfort.

You can't understand someone
unless you've lived their past
and with full contentment
realize how little you have,

and remember
when you need to be heard,
listen to yourself first
to be sure you're making sense
in such a nonsensical world.

This Is Not My Job, This Is Not My Problem

Monday, February 29, 2016

While I'm here struggling to see
what's beyond my front door,
much more falls around me.

So many questions left unanswered
in this life start with why.

Somewhere in my unspoken mind
my dilemma seems to be
from my window,

where I'm only able
to witness this world we built
crumble into dust;

I want to ask why,
when it became my job
to obtain any of the impossible,
did the initiative you failed to take
come crashing down on me?

March 2016

Superficial Impressions
Wednesday, March 2, 2016

The concern comes over me,
needles me in my good nature,
leaving behind the framework
for the frivolous to rip to pieces
with the fury of a savage.

I'm not a contestant
of your flawed perception.
I didn't ask for the verdict
you projected on me.

Why do I worry about your image of me,
when I couldn't see inside your mind
to get a glimpse of it?

Thoughts are what they are,
opinions without a voice
and some should stay unspoken.

To Move On
Tuesday, March 8, 2016

A deep breath,
a moment of silence,
and a sigh of relief.

At times, it's everything I need.

This Doesn't Even Scratch The Surface

Thursday, March 17, 2016

It's relentless and unforgiving,
it steals your conscious mind
and leaves your life at risk.

There the demons left me;
in a living nightmare,
hearing voices,
talking to the air,
walking round and round
up and down
the darkest halls of my life
and going nowhere.

I found myself searching for the will to live.

The chance to win the fight,
to prove I could defeat the unreal influence
which had come over me and shake
the frightening feelings of ending everything.

It's an endless battle, but it's one I'm willing to fight.

I can't let the destruction win
but if it takes me over a second time;

I pray to God to have the strength
to recall who I am,

and if my memory
doesn't serve me,
know I fought giving everything I had.

Know, I only left this life behind
because the choice wasn't mine to make,
the decision came from
the relentless and unforgiving
actions of an unfair mind.

I Have The Unusual Spring SAD

Tuesday, March 29, 2016

Spring has come with howling winds
and enough rain to fill my basement twice,
but a sunny day's out there somewhere.

With the lifeless-leafless trees,
the crows come to nest
on the bare branches the frost left behind.

In the center of my yard,
he sits staring straight up at the sky
as if his eye never saw a sunny sky .

Although I can't explain why,
its light wounds me.

Could it be the guilt of past spring seasons
which have come creeping upon me?

Does its disgrace pull me back
to an old emotional state?

I wish I could enjoy this season
as much as the rest,
but I'm stuck with lifeless trees
and enough rain to fill my basement twice.

April 2016

Self Destruction Is Not The Answer
Friday, April 8, 2016

It's happening all around you,
hopelessness sneaks its way into your home,
breaks down your door
and leaves you in the dark,
depressed, defeated, let down,
alone
to fend for yourself.

You're in the position to tell hopelessness
to hold on for a minute
while you take the time to remember how
fortunate, fulfilled, and fit
you are to fend for yourself despite
being alone.

The Rest Is History
Thursday, April 21, 2016

The emotions from one moment stay in my mind
as fresh as if they happened yesterday.

The dim-lit church gym,
the band playing loud
while my heart cracked,
broken by not one, but two.

It only takes one terrible action
to lose a lifelong friend,
we were not the same.

I didn't need you;
the lover,
or the friend,
who longed for each other.

Yet I cried the broken hearts cry, full of
bitterness, sadness, anger and envy,
full as it could be.

I look back on the day April 15, 2003,

as the ultimate example of what love shouldn't be
but lucky me, one year later on the same exact day
I came to see my husband to be.

Fifteen days later;

he didn't propose,
but admitted to marriage in the cards.

So here I live today,
in an amazing home with him,

and if love were a glass of wine
I'd be inebriated,
filling another to the brim.

Butting Heads With Myself

Tuesday, April 26, 2016

I miss the crickets chirping in the back of my mind
in the home we once knew.

Where our only company's;
the body of each other,
the warmth of the sunlight
and the silence from the streets
creeping through our window pane.

Company who gave us endless stories to tell
to a world full of possibilities and potential
which would root itself in my brain,
like ivy, impossible to remove.

I miss the cicadas roaring
outside my second story window
like aggressive waves in the sea.

No matter how alone I became,
they'd be there for me,
loud enough to overpower
each unsound thought come to mind.

The ivy has since been killed
by a remedy known as reality,
a place full of pesticides,
where my crickets and cicadas
had no chance to survive.

Reality left me;
desolate,
desperate,
downcast,
and knocked down
a notch or two
where my mind says I belong.

"I can't be anything I want to be,"
my mind would tell me,
I'm delusional for thinking
there's something out there meant for me.

So I guess I'm delusional
for thinking I'm right
where I'm meant to be.

May 2016

Accepting Yourself
Sunday, May 1, 2016

Who am I?

I'm a nobody,
blessed by the vast graveyard
of indifferent emotions
I've been handed.

Despite my eccentricities;
my failure to be courageous,
my lack of self-esteem,
and the hand dealt to me in life,

I'd rather be no one
but a nobody.

At times the truth screams
so loud at me, it says,
"I am who I am meant to be."

A Goodbye As I Try To Let It Go
Tuesday, May 17, 2016

When your tears drip acidic
and sting your cheeks
over the family
you haven't had the opportunity to have-

When do you stop grieving
over your losses?

Could it be your only choice to move on
into a world which seems so abysmal
without the ones you could've loved?

Stop Over-Thinking Things

Tuesday, May 17, 2016

You spend your entire existence
trying to gather your life in your arms,

but when there's no explanation
for an unsound mind
or unsound decisions made as a result,

it's a good time to let it fall to pieces
and let the dust settle.

Without the ability of clear thinking,
as long as you have a heartbeat
and a deep breath to take
at times, it's okay to let life fall to pieces.

My Night At The Roxbury

Sunday, May 22, 2016

My pen between my lips
as I decide how
I should say what
I'd want to say next,

or my teeth biting
the end of the eraser
until it seems to disappear.

My mind, once cluttered,
quiets to the soft hum
of traffic from a distance,
and when it's late,
it hears the train horn
screaming down the street.

A sudden memory of
how he once said he's
amazed by how we were able
to make ourselves heard.

It didn't matter if it meant,
we were tearing the foam
from the arms of the hospital chairs,
we felt as if it became
a safe place to be vulnerable.

I sensed a place of healing,
a place to build the foundation
for a well-balanced brain and well-being.

I said more
with the clutter in my head
trying to empty it out,
than I would when aware of my actions.

I wish I could obtain the same courage
as I had in an unsound state,
it's something critical which I lost.

June 2016

~~~~~~~

What If I Spoke My Mind All The Time?
Monday, June 13, 2016

When your thoughts decide to commentate,
your mind becomes a hard place to concentrate
on any single conversation.

Mine has spoken of snide comments,
I have kept all to myself.

"Some thoughts should
stay silent," I said.
I stick to that word like glue,

despite my mind
speaking so loud at times.
It's hard to even comprehend
the simplest of conversations.

In so few words I'm saying:
I am not a nice person in my mind,
I interrupt a lot, I'm conceited,
I'm the worst person I know.

My heart is full of good intentions,
my way to say I'm sorry for me
is to be kind
in my words and actions despite the trails
my thoughts may take me on.

The anxiety I feel for my mind
speaking out of turn is great,
because what I think isn't what I feel
and the guilt that comes as a result of doing so
is a weight that makes me wonder.

A Learning Experience

Tuesday, June 21, 2016

When there's something
stuck inside of you
which keeps creeping out,

do what you're able to do,
reason with yourself and say,
"We can work this out."

Let's move on;
let's live another day,
let's look forward.

Let's break free
from the ball and chain
which ties us to our twisted past
leaving us tangled
in the line of time
trying to escape.

We can cut and paste
ourselves a new perspective
on our past and call it.

A FRIEND

Tuesday, June 21, 2016

When you have one,
you have one for life. . .

Metaphorically-
an extra branch on the family tree.

Most importantly
one to swing on
which can also swing on you.

The Kind That Kill When The Going Gets Tough

Wednesday, June 22, 2016

Why do I cling
to your memory
so secure?

Let them go;

The utmost honest-
the silent ghost-
the liar which can't let up-
the quiet violent one.

They're only traits
in myself which I saw in you.

You left me,
on isolation island
where I faced the question,

what kind of companions could you be?

Sorry, But I Beg To Differ

Sunday, June 26, 2016

Honesty in small doses bleeds brutal in the end,
when lies in small doses don't exist, all lies are large.

When ignorance is bliss
we walk through with hope
as false as faulty doctrine;

from believing good deeds alone
will lead you into heaven up high,
to knowing good deeds alone
won't lead you there.

Our differences are something;
you can see in someone's eyes
and hear in their heart,

something from within which reflects
the character our creator has given us.

Remember, even in accordance with your beliefs,
everything we do to each other,
we do to Him as well.

August 2016

Do You Have A Death Wish?
Tuesday, August 2, 2016

To those who envy death,
do you count it as a wish
or a desire?

Is it that you'd like to see
the lives you've touched
or is it desperate plea
to run from life?

Why do you want so bad
to see what others feel the need
to say after you've gone?

You know,
if they don't say it
while the life runs through your blood
then they might not mean it
when the life runs out.

Say It Again And Again And Again
Wednesday, August 17, 2016

I wonder

if anyone worried about me,
if anyone had any words of wisdom
that I was unable to listen to
because I was busy
trying to be those words
for myself or another.

What did I miss
while I paused, preoccupied,
laboring with a thought
that lingered longer
than it should have?

I wish I could have you repeat
the words to me,
anything you've wanted to say
but in the end, much's mentioned
and not enough heard.

We missed our opportunity.

Who am I talking to?

Those who cared
that I tossed your feelings to the side
like children do broken toys,
but you meant everything to me
and you didn't stop to make me listen.

You gave up on me.

Equally
Monday, August 29, 2016

There are certain poets
I can't help but hate,
self righteous

indignant losers.

Yelling as if their anger and
emotional uprising is more than
just an adult temper tantrum
and means more the louder they speak,

or is super special in comparison
than anything, you've been through.

Boasting about,
like they're all that matters,
and only write about themselves,
their problems
and how they've been mistreated.

Sure, my opinion may be unpopular,
and it's typical for me to stay in silence,
so be ready to get offended, because
at times, it just needs to be said. . .

I get so sick of hearing
angry women complain in slam poetry
about how they're pissed off
because some loser wasn't man enough
to hold the door for them,

only to turn around in the same poem
to say they don't get treated with equality.

Let me explain something darling,
if you don't want an open door,
stop expecting one,
it sounds to me as if
he's treating you just how you wanted.

September 2016

<u>Another Set Of Shoes</u>

Friday, September 9, 2016

I've been given
a debatable mind,
honest,
at times, it's debatable
as to whether or not
it's even a mind at all,
but it thinks,
it even speaks for itself.

Either way,
it's about perspective,
a sense of persuasion.

Even in a messy mind like mine,
the ability to see,
yourself,
be seen,
and see through others

in a way which you've yet to see
may keep you from getting
hung up
on the one line you couldn't stand to see,
and help you see the story for its entirety.

Let the story live and die like us
and try fighting
for the other side
once in a while, with the intention
of sliding inside another mind.

It's Okay
Thursday, September 15, 2016

Dreams are the matter
we're made of
when our existence
feels like an illusion. . .

We seem
to tell ourselves;
it's a bad dream,
it'll be over when we wake.

At times, I wonder
if I'll wake up
when there's nothing to touch
to make us feel the same
as we did before we broke.

The good news,
we've never been broken for good
and if we have to be,
at least we're stranded on
shattered island together. . .
Right?

Something Like A Sonata
Wednesday, September 21, 2016

Listening to the crackling dust on a record
has me wishing I could have composed
a waterfall of keys that tap the strings
aggressively,
sadly,
sometimes even peacefully.

Smaller Than My Own Pinky

Thursday, September 22, 2016

When I was a single digit,
one summer my father found
a baby bird fallen
out of an evergreen.

My failed attempt to rescue the tiny bird,
smaller than my pinky
is an emotional upset
I do my best to make up for
with every life I save;

a dog at one end of my couch,
a mischief at the other,
a rabbit down the hall
beyond the kitchen
at the end of the stairway
where my basement belongs.

All at one point,
smaller than my pinky
but each a life worth saving,
because even I once was.

Transience

Thursday, September 22, 2016

You pour your soul
into a world that one day
won't remember you.

You come, sing your song
and dance, your job's done.

Live your life to disappear
but enjoy it while you're here.

Take a deep breath
and some day
let your life go in a
dizzying sigh.

No Matter How Deep You Dig

Friday, September 23, 2016

Grandma removed her face
last night before she went to bed.

It may have been a dream,
but she took it off as natural
as she would her dentures,
or hearing aids.

What was beneath the skin?

Nothing frightening,
but something I found
rather beautiful.

I found myself asking her
to take it off in an attempt
to better know what was underneath.

Raw and vulnerable to the elements,
with the ability to become dry and cracked.

Everything under that mask of skin
had become so familiar
with the seasons of this world
and the people in it.

The lesson learned;
at some point it's too late to
get to know a person.

I've Been There Before
Wednesday, September 28, 2016

No matter how loud you speak
some won't listen
and many times they're the ones
closest to you.

Busy listening to the one
with the anus made of gold,
but it doesn't matter what it's made of
it's not pretty
no matter how you dress it up.

At times, you need to look outside yourself
and just be okay with living in the shadow.
Pride is a powerful thing
but don't let it lead you to the same level
that led you in the shadow in the first place.

Your character is worth more
than you give it credit for
despite the indignant, sad, sullen, soul.

Be careful because your bitterness
just might bite you in the end.

Remember the shadow
isn't a bad place to be,
it's relatable,
it's a place so many have seen.

Yes, It Actually Happened
Wednesday, September 28, 2016

When I was alone,
I heard you speak to me
in every song the hospital radio played.

I've done the best I can,
I won't be here tomorrow,
goodbye is a second chance.

It wasn't ours,
it was a goodbye
to a set of circumstances
that grew old.

I thought my life was over,
just a whisper in my ear,
all I could remember was trying to take my life.

I didn't even realize I was alive,
so imagine not knowing
your spirit thrives
in your living, breathing body.

I mourned myself,
became another person,
first afraid, then bitter,
and every kind of person imaginable
but I grew stronger.

I wanted to go, needed to go
sick of swimming against the current;
letting my delusions drown me with fear,
anxiety, depression,
the feeling of living trapped in myself,
the surreal version of the world I saw,
and see on occasion today.

Let's bring back some bad memories
of actions with no explanations,
was I just dreaming?

I couldn't sleep,
I could never sleep.

So, how could that be?

Let Go Of My Arm

Thursday, September 29, 2016

You were possessive, aggressive, obsessive,
and I was so sixteen,
apprehensive, perceptive, susceptive.

I'll demonize you if I want to,
you went in for the hug I didn't want. . .

I pull as far from you as possible
because they warned me about you.
Yet you don't take the hint
and grab me, pulling me into an
awkward uncomfortable embrace.

So, as I walked off, upset,
you take my arm as if it's yours
and in one abrupt move, try to clear the air.

You're not making yourself look good to me,
or anyone around us,
so please stop trying, and leave me alone.

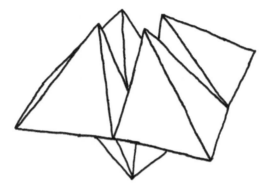

October 2016

Instant Gratification
Friday, October 7, 2016

It's a thing that luck grants you
and while certain things come easy,
and quick to some.

Certain things become
harder and harder to earn,
to see in others;

common sense,
common decency,
common courtesy.

It's important to remember yourself
through the thick of getting
what you want out of life,

before becoming prone to getting devoured
by your newly found fortune.

Nostalgia Bites

Friday, October 14, 2016

Sinking into the past
seems to be all I do,
at times there's nothing
left to think about
but the comfort of a few
good times gone by.

They become crowded
by the feeling of nothing left
to look forward to,

then flood in the memories amiss.

I don't miss;
I don't look at our photos,
I don't read the memoirs,
I don't search for you
like you do me.

I remember different from you;
where you remember happy,
I remember angst and uneasiness,
where you remember love,
I remember babble and hearsay,
where you remember friendship,
I remember a spiteful and evil eye.

My future and today are all I have,
they're the only friends I need
that haven't been here since square one.

So The Cycle Continues
Saturday, October 22, 2016

Twisted and torn is the page that read;
I don't belong-
at least I thought my family felt that way.

Turn the page and tear it out;
tattered
is the page that read I've got no stability.

What do you know about mental health?

It took ten years to heal, and more than half of them
didn't even know what healing was yet.

See, you helped me with none of that.

I remember the first day depression hit me-
it was more than the school bully tugging on my hair.

I remember my first feeling of complete hopelessness
as I first felt what death was.

Nine years old and it's the only thought
that screamed to me so loud in my life,

"What's the point in anything?"
I said to myself so torn with fear,
"I'm going to die either way. . .

So die."

-I told myself to;

and my first attempt at self harm,
before I even knew what it was;

Depression came,
straightened out the end of an old metal coat hanger,
and scraped my skin until it welted over.

Swollen, tender and red but no blood
-only nine years old.

It just felt better. . .

and of course it escalated later
to further self harm of all different forms,
but the worst kinds were the ones of the mind;

Poking and prodding,
tearing me down
when all I was trying to do was

survive.

I wanted to thrive,
sure I could go out,
feel good with friends,
but then when left alone,
here comes the thought;

"What's the point?"

And it's so sudden,
I'm dying once more.

Easier Said Than Done
Tuesday, October 25, 2016

At times;
it's just a looming cloud overhead,
or a rain that brings a shallow flood,
becoming a typhoon that
consumes your entire city.

If you can look past that wreckage,
to see that we're all just a drop of rain
in the bucket at the end of the day;

One day you'll be able
to see the sun again.

November 2016

<u>Art</u>

Tuesday, November 15, 2016

It's impossible to comprehend
all that's been spoken to it,

we can commiserate,
bask in its inevitable glory;

Despite the opinions,
the paint, color,
or any other medium,
the potential energy
drained on that canvas
doesn't see those limitations

-our imaginations don't
see those restrictions either.

It's an intimate part of somebody.

Life

Tuesday, November 22, 2016

People pretend
it's all fluff and feathers,

it's not a pillow,
and for humanity
as a whole

it's somewhere between
a rock and a hard place.

December 2016

So Be Gracious
Tuesday, December 6, 2016

Why's a world so immoral,
so willing to talk about the corruption
which we're slow to sink in?

Sinking seems
to become second nature.

Yet when it comes
to having a conversation
about our potential creator,
rather than of agreeing to disagree
or walking out with kindness

-someone gets stuck
feeling left in the dark.

With the stumbling we're doing,
it's a surprise we don't get up
with a mouthful of dirt more.

Why does the world
have to look so
bleak for everyone else when you're
able to see your salvation?

You need to realize,
for everyone else
nothing changes
-life stays the same.
They don't see the world
the way you do.

So I Try Not To Think About It
Thursday, December 8, 2016

He looks at me with his tired eyes
as he drifts off to sleep.

He's dying of age, but you know everyone does,
and I know one day his will hit me harder than any other.

I look back to yesterday, me, on the edge of 16,
and today you're 30.

A decade has passed,
but it's as if yesterday we were meeting
for the first time on the porch of my parents' house,
then walking around with my friends and I
as if we owned the town;

when the only item we owned
were the disposable cameras in our hands
before everything turned digital on us.

Time goes by too fast to force yourself to own
each bit of the animosity you and I
have been able to throw out over the years,
no matter who you may be;
brothers or sisters,
friends,
enemies, and even us lovers.

Keep in mind, despite our love or disdain,
our bodies won't last eternal
and one day we're likely to throw a shovel of dirt
over another's grave.

I hope the time's far from near,
but I know one day everyone will have tired eyes.

Questions For My Multiple Personalities

Thursday, December 15, 2016

Remember when we put our faith into paper fortunes?

Back when he said she said
defined our self-worth,
and focusing on our losses
left us with nothing left to gain.

Remember when we had no personalities,
and passed notes to prattle on
about our petty lives?

Where's the observant one?

Could he be busy writing notes
to himself about how he feels life should be?

So busy seeing how the world turns
and missing out on experiencing
how relationships form.

Why did the reliant one take over?
So focused on another's assessment of himself,
full of vacant jubilation,
yet so far from full of himself.

He's the one who can't be alone,
the incredible lost one,
annihilated by loneliness.

Where did this strong one
surprise me from?

The one who's apprehensive, protective,
with an inhibition a bit strong
to live a pleasant life.

Why's he so hard to handle?

Stepping in
at the most inopportune time.

Why doesn't he step up when I need him?

Be Yourself

Sunday, December 18, 2016

You act so counterfeit,
so fictitious,
so sunken in
to your so called sparkling,
yet incredible unoriginal
presence you persuade this world
to put their faith in.

Who do you claim to be;

the person who talked to me for hours
about the substance of our lives,

or the one who speaks of shallow wit?

Reality told me today-
what substance once existed,
I can no longer find.

Quit covering yourself in dimwitted
attempts at being another self
and don't deny yourself the chance to.

I Never Told You That

Sunday, December 25, 2016

You don't have to like me
-who says I'm being relatable?

You don't have to respect me
-who says I've earned it?

You don't have to hear me
-who says I'm worth listening to?